Tales of Famous Americans

Tales of Famous Americans

Connie and Peter Roop

Illustrations by Charlie Powell

SCHOLASTIC REFERENCE
An imprint of
SCHOLASTIC

Roop, Connie.

Tales of famous Americans/Connie and Peter Roop; illustrations by Charlie Powell.

p. cm.

Includes index.

ISBN-13: 978-0-439-64116-6 (alk. paper)

ISBN-10: 0-439-64116-0 (alk. .paper)

1. Celebrities—United States—Biography—Juvenile Literature. 2. United States—Biography—Juvenile Literature. I. Roop, Peter. II. Powell, Charlie. III. Title.

CT217.R66 2007

973.09'9--dc22

2007061714

10 9 8 7 6 5 4 3 2 1   07 08 09 10 11

Printed in Singapore

First printing, October 2007

Illustrations by Charlie Powell
Book design by Tatiana Sperhacke

PHOTO CREDITS

Pages 2-3: © George Sullivan; pages 8-9: © E. O. Hoppé/CORBIS; pages 14-15: © CORBIS; pages 20-21: © Tennessee State Library & Archives; Pages 26-27: © White House Historical Society; pages 32-33: © Peter Steiner/Alamy; pages 38-39: © George Sullivan; pages 44-45: © CORBIS; pages 50-51: © Collections of Henry Ford Museum & Greenfield Village; pages 56-57: © Indiana Historical Society Library; pages 62-63: © Museum of Flight/CORBIS; pages 68-69: © Bettmann/CORBIS; pages 74-75: © Bettmann/CORBIS; pages 80-81: © AP/Wide World Photos; pages 86-87: © 1976 George Ballis/TAKE STOCK; pages 92-93: © Steve J. Sherman Photography LLC, NY, NY; pages 98-99: © Bongarts/Getty Images.

Contents

Pocahontas

1595–1617

Pocahontas, a member of the Powhatan tribe, was born in Virginia in 1595 or 1596. No one knows her exact birth date. The baby girl was named Matoaka, which means "playful."

Her father, Powhatan, was the chief of many villages. Powhatan had twenty-seven children, but Matoaka was his favorite child. Chief Powhatan nicknamed his daughter Pocahontas, which means "lively and cheerful." Soon everyone was calling her Pocahontas.

Pocahontas

was treated like a princess. She practiced standing tall and straight like her father. She didn't have to do the usual chores girls her age did. Pocahontas learned right from wrong by listening to her people's stories and watching her elders. She was taught that too much talking was rude.

In 1607, when Pocahontas was eleven, her world changed forever. Three English ships sailed up the James River in Virginia. The Englishmen built a fort they named Jamestown near where Pocahontas lived.

At first, Chief Powhatan was friendly so that the English would trade with his tribe. But problems arose between the Native Americans and the English. Trade stopped. The English stayed inside their fort. Many died from disease and hunger.

Finally, the English sent Captain John Smith, a brave soldier, to meet Chief Powhatan in his longhouse. Men and women from his tribe joined the chief in a feast welcoming John Smith.

John Smith wrote an exciting account about that night years after it happened. We may never know if all of the facts in Smith's story are true, but according to Smith, this is what happened after the feast.

An English ship

After eating, Chief Powhatan ordered two big stones to be carried into his longhouse. John Smith was dragged to the stones. He was forced to put his head on one stone. Then two warriors raised their clubs to kill John Smith!

Suddenly, Pocahontas ran to John Smith. With her body, she protected him from the deadly clubs. She didn't want him to be hurt.

Chief Powhatan, seeing how his daughter had protected him, ordered that John Smith be set free. Powhatan told Smith they were now friends. Smith would be adopted into the tribe and would be like a big brother to Pocahontas.

John Smith and Pocahontas became good friends. She brought food to the starving English. She taught John words in her language like *moccasin*, *tuffan* (beds), and *pokatawer* (fire). John carefully wrote these words in a book. Before long, Pocahontas and John were *mawchick chammay*, best friends.

Pocahontas made other English friends, too. Boys taught her to turn somersaults and cartwheels. They taught her English words.

But the troubles between the Powhatan and the English continued.

Chief Powhatan wanted the English to leave his lands.

John Smith captured some Native American men. Pocahontas begged him to free the men. Finally, Captain Smith let the men go.

A house in the Jamestown settlement

Chief Powhatan then planned to capture Captain Smith. Pocahontas helped him escape.

Then John Smith was badly burned in an accident. He sailed home to England to recover. Pocahontas believed her friend had died.

More English people settled in Virginia. Life was hard for them. There was rarely enough food. The Native Americans attacked them.

In 1612, Captain Samuel Argall tricked Pocahontas into coming aboard his ship, where he captured her! He told Chief Powhatan that he wouldn't let Pocahontas go until the Native Americans stopped attacking the English and returned English weapons that had been taken.

Powhatan loved his daughter, but he wanted the English to leave even more. He didn't rescue Pocahontas!

Pocahontas was sent to live at Rock Hall, a farm owned by an Englishman. She dressed in English clothes. She studied the Bible and became a Christian. Pocahontas was given an English name, Rebecca.

During this time, Pocahontas met John Rolfe, a farmer. John Rolfe and Pocahontas fell in love and married. Chief Powhatan sent Pocahontas a string of pearls as a wedding gift.

Pocahontas's string of pearls

Now that his daughter had married an Englishman, Chief Powhatan promised peace. This was called the Peace of Pocahontas.

In 1615, Pocahontas had a baby named Thomas. The next year, Pocahontas and her family sailed to England, where she was treated like a princess. She wore beautiful clothes at special dinners and dances. Pocahontas even met the king and queen of England.

London was too damp, dirty, and crowded for Pocahontas. She became ill, so the Rolfes moved to the country. Pocahontas was much happier living where the air was cleaner and where she was surrounded by trees.

One day, Pocahontas had a big surprise. John Smith knocked on her door. Pocahontas was happy to see her friend alive. They talked for a long time. After his visit, however, John Smith never saw Pocahontas again.

John Rolfe decided to return to Virginia, but Pocahontas was still sick. Before she reached the ocean, she grew worse. She was taken off the ship. A doctor came, but he was too late. Pocahontas died in 1617. She was only twenty-one years old.

Pocahontas was buried in Gravesend, England, far from her Virginia home. Today a statue there marks her grave.

Thomas Rolfe

Benjamin Franklin

1706–1790

Benjamin, the fifteenth of the seventeen Franklin children, was born on January 17, 1706, in Boston, Massachusetts.

Josiah Franklin, Ben's father, made candles and soap. He struggled to feed, clothe, and educate his large family.

Benjamin

was a curious child. He explored his home on Milk Street. He asked many questions about what he saw. He did chores around the crowded Franklin home.

Ben liked to play, too. He loved swimming. One day, Ben had an idea. He knew ducks swam fast with their webbed feet. He invented paddles for his hands and feet so he could swim faster. Another time he experimented with a kite. As he floated, Ben let his kite pull him around the pond!

Ben especially enjoyed reading. He said, "I do not remember when I could not read." He borrowed every book he could find.

Ben went to school when he was eight. He did so well that he skipped a grade. When he was ten, Ben left school to make candles and soap with his father. He didn't like the hot, hard work. He wanted to be a sailor, but his father said no.

Ben watched men at their jobs. Should he be a tailor, a carpenter, a bricklayer, or a blacksmith? Then his father had an idea. Ben liked to work with his hands and he liked words. Ben should become a printer!

Making candles

10

When Ben was twelve, his brother James agreed to teach him how to be a printer. James wouldn't pay Ben, but he would give his brother food and a bed. Working as an apprentice in the printing shop was perfect for Ben. He enjoyed printing books and newspapers.

Ben began secretly writing stories for the newspaper his brother printed. Ben signed his stories with a name he made up: Silence Dogood. People laughed at what Silence Dogood said, and more papers than ever were sold. James was very happy about the success of Silence Dogood, but he wondered who the mysterious writer was.

One day, James discovered that Ben was really Silence Dogood. He got quite angry at Ben for tricking him. After that, working for James was difficult for Ben. When he was seventeen, Ben ran away to Philadelphia, Pennsylvania.

Ben easily found work in a printing shop. He quickly earned a reputation as an excellent, dependable printer.

Still, Ben was not happy. He wanted to be his own boss, so he started a printing business in 1728. Ben went to bed early, got up early, worked hard, and made his printing business successful.

Printing press

Ben wrote and printed *Poor Richard's Almanack*, a small book of recipes, jokes, weather predictions, and wise sayings. One of *Poor Richard's* sayings was: "Early to bed, early to rise, makes a man healthy, wealthy, and wise." *Poor Richard* was very popular and made Ben a wealthy man. Now he had enough money to stop working and to do scientific experiments.

One day, Ben saw a man experimenting with electricity. He became very curious about electricity because no one really knew what it was. Ben began his own experiments with electricity. He invited people to watch his experiments.

Ben did his most famous experiment in 1752. He wanted to prove his idea that lightning was electricity. One stormy day, he flew a kite in a thunderstorm. He had tied a metal key to the end of his kite string. Lightning flashed. Electricity charged down the kite string, struck the key, and sparked Ben's knuckle.

Ben was right! Lightning was electricity. He was lucky that the lightning didn't kill him. Ben became world famous as the man who tamed lightning. Busy Ben also enjoyed inventing useful things. He invented a battery, bifocal glasses, and the Franklin stove.

Ben was very proud of his stove because it didn't cause smoke to come into rooms like other stoves did. Ben's stove also burned much less wood. Ben could have earned money from his inventions, but he gave his ideas away because he wanted to help people.

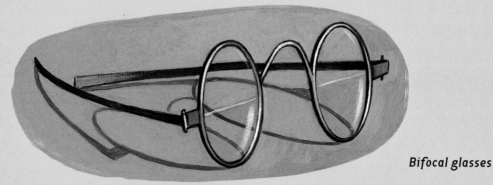

Bifocal glasses

When the American Revolution began, Ben helped the thirteen colonies become a new nation. He signed the Declaration of Independence. It said the thirteen colonies were now the United States of America.

The United States needed friends to win the war against England. Ben went to France in 1776 to ask the French people to help the struggling United States. Ben used his charm and his powerful words to talk the French into fighting England. In 1778, Ben signed the treaty with France that brought them into the war on the side of the United States. With the help of French money, ships, and guns, the United States won the war.

Ben's work wasn't over. Now the young United States had to write its own laws. They put laws into a document called the Constitution. As usual, Ben was there to help serve his country. He helped write the Constitution at the Pennsylvania State House in Philadelphia. He signed it, too.

Ben kept sharing his talents until April 17, 1790, when he died peacefully in his sleep. People around the world were sad when Ben Franklin—printer, inventor, scientist, friend, and leader—died. Ben was buried in Philadelphia, the city he loved.

Pennsylvania State House

George Washington
1732–1799

Augustine Washington wrote his newborn son's name in the family
Bible: *George Washington*. George was born on February 22, 1732.
His proud parents took him around the colony of Virginia for family
and friends to admire.

George

Washington grew tall and strong. He loved the farms and forests of Virginia. He swam and fished in the Potomac River. He wrestled and raced with his friends.

As their "general," George led his "soldier" friends in many imaginary battles. His friends admired George and followed him everywhere.

By the time he was ten years old, George hunted turkey and deer for his family to eat. He galloped down dusty roads on fast horses to visit his friends. He watched his father keep track of the things he bought and sold. George especially liked to help his father add, subtract, multiply, and divide.

Compass

George used his math skills to survey land. Surveying is measuring land and making a map of the land so people know what land they own. When he was a teenager, George made a map of his farm. He signed the map with his initials, *GW*.

George's surveying trips took him deeper into the wilderness. He camped and took care of himself in dangerous situations. With the money he earned, George began to buy land he liked. By the time he was twenty years old, George Washington owned more than two thousand acres of fine farmland and several slaves.

George worked hard to learn new things, to take care of himself, and to make himself a better person. He even wrote down 110 rules to help himself. One rule said, "Keep your nails clean and short." Another rule was "Be careful to keep your promises." All his life, George tried to follow his 110 rules, but sometimes this was difficult for determined George Washington.

George often dreamed about what he would be as an adult. Would he be a farmer like his father? Would he be a sailor like his friend? Would he be a soldier like his brother Lawrence?

When he was twenty-one, George had a chance to become a soldier. Men listened to him and looked up to him even though he was young. George was a major in the British army. He did so well that he was promoted to colonel.

In 1754, Colonel Washington and his soldiers were fighting against French soldiers in the French and Indian War. George Washington lost the battle and had to surrender. He learned an important lesson. George never surrendered again!

After the costly war with the French was over, England's King George III told the thirteen American colonies they had to pay for it. He told the Americans they must pay taxes on things like paper and tea. The Americans said no. The British said yes.

In 1775, British soldiers shot American soldiers at Lexington and Concord in Massachusetts. The American patriots needed a general to lead them against the British. They chose tall, strong, and determined George Washington.

In 1776, the American colonies declared their independence from Britain. They were now the thirteen United States of America. The American Revolutionary War had begun.

Box of tea

The British had the strongest army and biggest navy in the world. How could the thirteen states defeat them?

The United States had General George Washington.

At first, General Washington lost some battles, but he did not surrender. On December 26, 1776, General Washington won a battle at Trenton, New Jersey. Soon he won another battle at Princeton, New Jersey.

General Washington's trifold hat

Could the United States really win its independence? People around the world wondered. George Washington believed it could, so he did not give up. He wouldn't let his men give up either, even after they lost battles, even after suffering the long, cold winter at Valley Forge, Pennsylvania, in 1777–1778.

For three more years, the two armies fought. In 1781, General Washington defeated British troops at Yorktown, Virginia.

By 1783, the United States had won the war!

The young country needed a strong leader to help it become a strong nation. George Washington was the best choice.

In 1789, George Washington became the first president of the United States.

President Washington served his country for eight years. He worked hard and was respected by Americans and people from other countries, too. By 1797, however, President Washington was ready to be Farmer Washington.

President Washington went home to his farm at Mount Vernon, Virginia.

One cold, rainy December day in 1799, George was riding his horse around Mount Vernon. Ever since he was young, George had enjoyed riding horses. After being wet all day, however, George ended up getting a terrible cold.

On December 14, 1799, George Washington died.

One friend said that George Washington was "first in war, first in peace, and first in the hearts of his countrymen."

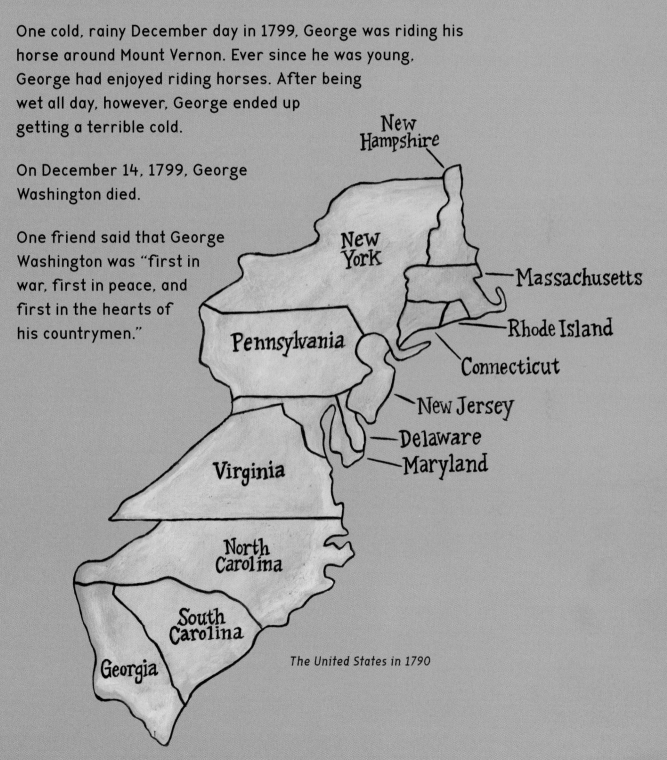

The United States in 1790

PIONEER, STATESMAN

Davy Crockett

1786–1836

David Crockett was born in a log cabin in eastern Tennessee on August 17, 1786.

Davy's father ran a small tavern that served traveling traders and cattle herders. When Davy was old enough, he helped his father by taking care of the travelers' horses. He chopped wood, milked cows, and chased raccoons out of the Crockett cornfield.

Davy found time to explore the forest near his home. He learned to mimic birdcalls. He imitated a bear's growl, a wolf's howl, and a panther's scream. Davy hunted with bow and arrows, threw tomahawks, and slipped silently through the woods.

When Davy was eight, his father gave him his first rifle. Davy was allowed only one bullet at a time because bullets and gunpowder were expensive.

At first, when Davy went hunting, he returned empty-handed. But with his excellent eyesight and steady aim, Davy soon brought home squirrels, deer, and turkeys for the cooking pot.

Davy's life of adventure began when he was twelve. He took a job helping a farmer drive a herd of cattle. They traveled four hundred miles on muddy trails, over misty mountains, and across rushing rivers to Virginia. Davy walked the entire way from Tennessee to Virginia. Davy missed his family, but he enjoyed the chance to explore the country.

Cattle

Davy was paid six dollars for all of his hard work and returned home. But Davy didn't stay home for long. He got into a fight at school. Knowing his father would be very angry, Davy ran away and joined another cattle drive.

For the next few years, Davy worked on farms, drove wagons, and made beaver hats. His parents didn't know where Davy was. Finally, he headed home.

When Davy entered the Crockett tavern, no one recognized the tall, strong young man in a coonskin cap. Then his sister realized that the handsome stranger was their long-lost Davy!

When Davy was just about twenty, he married Polly Finley and settled down to farm. Before long, Davy, Polly, and their two sons moved farther west to find better land.

Davy explored, roamed, and hunted in the wilderness. He earned the reputation as the best hunter around.

Hunters told tall tales about Davy. One said Davy just had to grin at a raccoon for the raccoon to surrender. Another told how Davy shot seventeen geese with one bullet.

In 1813, Davy joined the militia as a scout to fight Native Americans who were battling to save their lands. Davy, who loved the land like the Native Americans did, understood why they fought so hard. Later, Davy tried to help his Native American friends keep their homes.

Davy became so well known that he was elected to the Tennessee government to make laws. Davy's friends encouraged him to run for the

Raccoon surrendering

U.S. Congress. Davy agreed. During his campaign, people joked about Davy's many adventures. They said he was so popular that even the crickets chirped, "CR-K-TT!" and the bullfrogs croaked, "CRO-O-CKETT-TT!" Davy won the election.

Davy was nicknamed the "Coonskin Congressman" in Washington, D.C., because he always wore his coonskin cap. Davy's motto was: "Be always sure you're right, and go ahead!" He worked to help farmers who owned small farms. He also tried to stop the Native Americans from being moved off their lands. Many folks in Tennessee were angry because they wanted the Native Americans' lands for themselves.

A bullfrog croaking for Crockett

Davy lost the next Tennessee election, but he was popular in other states. People talked about electing him president of the United States. In 1835, as the first step to that goal, Davy ran for Congress again from Tennessee. Unfortunately, he lost and gave up his hopes to be president.

After his defeat, Davy announced, "I'm going to Texas!" He was tired of Tennessee politics and was eager for new adventures in his life. Texas was trying to break away from Mexico, so Davy decided to join the Texans in their fight for independence.

A large Mexican army commanded by General Santa Anna marched to Texas to end the rebellion. Davy and two hundred men turned the ruins of an old mission building into a fort they called the Alamo.

The Alamo

In March 1836, the Mexican army surrounded the Alamo. Davy knew it would be a fight to the death. He tried to keep up his men's spirits by singing, playing a fiddle, and telling stories.

Early on the morning of March 6, more than five thousand Mexican soldiers attacked the Alamo. Davy and the men fought bravely, but they were outnumbered. When the battle ended, Davy Crockett was dead, his coonskin cap beside him.

Davy Crockett, hunter, pioneer, scout, storyteller, politician, and soldier, gave his life to help Texas gain its independence. Folks across America honored Davy and the men who died by his side, pledging to always "Remember the Alamo!"

Abraham Lincoln

1809–1865

A blazing fire warmed the Lincoln family's one-room log cabin on February 12, 1809. Nancy Lincoln rocked her newborn son. Tom Lincoln, the proud father, brought them a bearskin blanket. Sarah stared at her wrinkle-faced baby brother.

"What are you going to call him?" asked Dennis Hanks, Nancy's young cousin.

"Abraham, after his grandfather Abraham Lincoln."

Dennis exclaimed, "He'll never amount to much!"

Abraham Lincoln's family struggled to earn a living farming in the Kentucky wilderness. When Abe was two, the Lincolns moved to Knob Creek. Five years later, in 1816, the Lincolns moved to Indiana.

Young Abe grew tall and strong. He helped his father plow, plant, and harvest their crops. He chopped down trees, cut firewood, and split fence rails. Abe fed the farm animals and carried heavy buckets of water for his mother.

When his chores were finished, **Abraham** played with his sister, Sarah, or his friend Austin Gollaher. One day, Abe fell into a rushing creek, but he couldn't swim! Fortunately, Austin rescued Abe.

Abe enjoyed learning. He learned his ABC's, arithmetic, and how to print his name. Abe wrote this in his copybook:

Abraham Lincoln his hand and pen

He will be good but God knows when.

Split-rail fence

28

Like many pioneer children, Abe went to school only when he wasn't needed on the farm. Sometimes there was no teacher in the wilderness, so the school didn't open. Altogether, Abe only had one full year of school. Abe joked that he went to school by "littles," a little here and a little there.

Abe loved to read. He took a book when he worked in the fields. He read at night by the flickering firelight. Once Abe borrowed a book and accidentally got it wet. He worked for three days to pay for the book!

When Abe was twenty-one, he helped his family move to Illinois. Having worked hard for his father ever since he was a boy, Abe decided he was now old enough to earn his own living. He went to New Salem to work in a general store.

Once Abe charged a woman six cents too much for tea. He walked six miles to return her money. Abe was earning his nickname, "Honest Abe."

The storekeeper gave Abe an adventurous job. He floated a log raft loaded with hogs, lumber, and meat to New Orleans down the Mississippi and Ohio Rivers. There he saw a slave market in which African-Americans were being bought and sold. Abe never forgot this sad scene.

General store

People liked honest Abraham Lincoln. In 1834, he was elected to the Illinois State Legislature to make laws. Abe decided to become a lawyer. He couldn't afford college so he taught himself the law.

In 1842, Abe married Mary Todd. The Lincolns bought a home in Springfield, Illinois, where Abe had his law office. The Lincolns lived in Springfield for seventeen years. Their sons Eddie, Willie, and Tad were also born in Springfield.

In 1846, Abe was elected to the U.S. House of Representatives in Washington, D.C. The House of Representatives helps make laws for the whole country. Abe worked hard for two years. In 1848, he decided to leave politics and return home.

During Abe's life, new states were being added to the United States. The southern states, with slavery, wanted these new states to allow slavery. The northern states, without slavery, wanted the new states to be free. The debate raged across America.

Abe knew slavery was wrong and spoke against it, saying, "I believe the government cannot endure half-slave and half-free."

Abe changed his mind about politics. He ran for the U.S. Senate in 1858, but lost. Abraham Lincoln's honest voice, however, had been heard.

In 1860 Abe ran for president of the United States and won! He would be the sixteenth president.

Abraham Lincoln presidential election medallion

In 1861, the southern states left the United States to create their own nation. President Lincoln said they couldn't do this, even if it took a war to keep the country united.

On April 12, 1861, the Civil War began. President Lincoln was saddened by Americans fighting Americans, but he was determined to save the whole United States.

President Lincoln signed the Emancipation Proclamation. This important document freed slaves in the southern states on January 1, 1863. Later that year, President Lincoln gave his famous Gettysburg Address, honoring the soldiers who had died fighting at Gettysburg, Pennsylvania.

In 1864, Abe was reelected president. When the Civil War ended on April 9, 1865, President Lincoln's dream that the states would be united again came true. He asked all Americans to work together to heal the wounds of war.

President Lincoln didn't live to see this happen. On April 14, 1865, John Wilkes Booth shot President Lincoln while he watched a play at Ford's Theater in Washington, D.C. Fifty-six-year-old Abraham Lincoln died the next morning.

Abraham Lincoln, born in a log cabin, grew up to live in the White House and become one of our most popular and respected presidents.

Ford's Theater

17

Entrance At
39 Madison St.

Susan B. Anthony 1820–1906 and
Elizabeth Cady Stanton 1815–1902

Susan B. Anthony was born near Adams, Massachusetts, on February 15, 1820. She was the second of the eight Anthony children.

Susan's parents were members of the Quaker religion. Their strong beliefs influenced Susan. As Quakers, the Anthonys believed that men and women were equals. They raised their daughters and sons to believe the same thing. Susan would fight all her life for such equality.

Susan was a bright, shy child. She learned to read when she was four. The Anthonys felt that everyone must be useful to the world. Her mother taught Susan how to sew, clean, cook, wash dishes, and do laundry. These were typical household chores for a farm girl like Susan.

Because of their religious beliefs, Quakers didn't allow their children to have toys, play music, dance, or join games.

In 1826, the Anthony family moved to New York. When Susan was older, her father ran a cotton mill. He hired young women to work in his mill. He paid them fair wages. When Susan was eleven years old, she worked in the mill for two weeks. Susan spent every penny she earned on three blue teacups for her overworked mother.

Susan became a teacher when she was fifteen. By the time she was seventeen, she was paid $1.50 a week. She was upset, though, because male teachers were paid $6.00 a week, four times what women teachers earned! Susan knew this was unfair, but there was nothing she could do about it.

Susan's gift for her mother: three blue teacups

Five years before Susan was born, the Cady family welcomed their eighth child. Elizabeth Cady was born on November 12, 1815. She grew up in the finest house in Johnstown, New York.

Elizabeth was a happy, intelligent, outgoing child. She had her own opinions. Sometimes she got into trouble for her strong beliefs. Elizabeth stood up against her mother when she made all the Cady girls wear red dresses. She was punished for speaking up.

Elizabeth's father, Daniel, was a judge. He also gave people legal advice. Elizabeth learned early in her life that some laws were not fair. This made her angry. She was determined to do something to change them.

One day, a widow named Mrs. Campbell came to see Judge Daniel Cady. She was upset. When her husband died, she lost her family's farm. Mrs. Campbell's parents had given her the farm before she married. Now she wanted the farm back. Judge Cady told her that, as a woman, she had given up her rights to the farm when she married. New York State law said the farm legally belonged to her husband. When Mr. Campbell died, the farm went to another owner because Mr. Campbell had owed him money.

Elizabeth was so angry, she told her father she was going to cut out all of the unfair laws from his law books!

Mr. Stanton's law books

Her only brother died when Elizabeth was eleven. Judge Cady was heartbroken. He loved his daughters, but had all of his hopes on his son. Judge Cady told Elizabeth, "Oh, my daughter, I wish you were a boy!"

Elizabeth cried, "I will try to be all my brother was."

And she did. Elizabeth became a tomboy, jumping ditches and riding horses. She was able to compete with boys in school and beat them.

When Elizabeth was fifteen, she decided to go to college. But no college in America allowed women to enter. Elizabeth knew that women could not be doctors, lawyers, or ministers. Even if a woman had a job, she had to give all of her money to her husband or father.

Elizabeth was upset because women couldn't vote to change the unfair laws, either.

VOTES FOR WOMEN

A banner demanding "Votes for Women"

In 1840, Elizabeth married Henry Stanton. But she refused to give up her name. She chose to be called Elizabeth Cady Stanton.

In 1848, thirty-two-year-old Elizabeth decided to take action against laws that were unfair to women. She helped organize the first women's rights convention in Seneca Falls, New York. Elizabeth modeled the convention's statement after the Declaration of Independence. She felt all men and women were created equal. Elizabeth urged the women and men at the convention to demand women's right to vote. The women and men working so everyone could vote were called suffragists. Both Susan and Elizabeth were well-known suffragists.

In 1851, Elizabeth met Susan B. Anthony. For the next fifty years, Elizabeth and Susan were close friends. Together they fought for equal rights.

First, Susan and Elizabeth put their energies into ending slavery. Elizabeth wrote speeches. Susan organized meetings against slavery. When slavery ended after the Civil War, Susan and Elizabeth worked for equal rights for women. They especially wanted women to have the right to vote. They traveled, gave speeches, and wrote books and newspaper articles. Susan even went to jail for trying to vote when she was told she couldn't. They knew it would be a long battle. But, as Susan said, "Failure is impossible."

Finally, in 1919, the Nineteenth Amendment was passed, giving women the right to vote. Unfortunately, neither Elizabeth Cady Stanton nor Susan B. Anthony lived to see that historic day. Elizabeth had died in 1902. Susan had died in 1906.

In 1979, to honor her fight for equal rights, Susan became the first woman ever to be featured on a U.S. coin. The coin is the Susan B. Anthony silver dollar.

Susan B. Anthony silver dollar

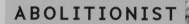

ABOLITIONIST

Harriet Tubman

1821–1913

Harriet Tubman was born in Maryland in 1821. Harriet's exact birth date is not known because she was born a slave and, in those days, slave birthdays were rarely recorded. Harriet was owned by her mother's master.

Harriet's parents named her Araminta Ross. Araminta was shortened to Minty.

Minty was one of eleven children. She slept in a wooden cradle made by her father. Her parents struggled to keep their large family together even though they lived on different farms and were owned by different masters.

Minty's parents worried that their children would be sold to other masters far away. This fear came true when two of Minty's sisters were sold.

When Minty was five, her master rented her to another family. Little Minty had to do house chores and take care of a baby. At night, she slept on the floor beside the baby's cradle. When the baby cried, Minty rocked the cradle. If she wasn't fast enough to quiet the baby, she was whipped. Once Minty had five lashes before breakfast! She carried scars from that whipping all her life.

When she was seven, Minty stole a lump of sugar from a bowl. She had never tasted sugar before. She hoped her mistress wouldn't see her, but the woman did! Minty ran away to escape a beating. She hid in a pigpen for five days, fighting the pigs for food scraps. Starving and miserable, Minty returned to her mistress and her punishment.

Cradle

Minty worked in the fields when she was twelve. She enjoyed being outside where she grew strong and healthy. She lifted heavy barrels, chopped wood, and hauled logs. She plowed, planted, and harvested crops. Minty wore her hair wrapped in a bandanna or a hat, a habit she kept for the rest of her life.

When Minty was thirteen, she tried to help a slave who was in trouble. She stood between the slave and his boss. The angry boss threw a heavy weight at the slave. The weight hit Minty instead and fractured her skull!

She took months to recover from her horrible head wound. Minty's injury bothered her until the day she died.

Minty's bandanna

In 1844, Minty married John Tubman, a free black man. Five years later, when her master died, Minty learned she was going to be sold. She made up her mind. She said, "There was one of two things I had a right to, liberty or death; if I could not have one, I would have the other." Minty decided to run away to the North where she could be free. Her husband refused to go with her because he was already free and did not want to make the risky journey.

In September 1849, Minty escaped. She slept during the day and traveled at night. Minty knew the North Star would guide her to freedom. Along the way, people helped her by giving her food and shelter. Many of these people belonged to the Underground Railroad. This railroad wasn't one with train tracks. Instead it was a group of people who helped slaves escape to freedom. They did this by guiding the slaves along secret routes to safe places, called "stations," until they reached a free state in the North.

Later Minty said, "When I found I had crossed that line [into Pennsylvania, which didn't allow slavery], I looked at my hands to see if I was the same person. . . . I felt like I was in heaven." To honor her freedom, Minty changed her name to her mother's name, Harriet.

Back in Maryland, a reward was promised for Minty's capture and return.

Harriet was never captured, but she did return to Maryland even though it was very dangerous for her to do so. Over the next ten years, Harriet helped other African-Americans escape slavery, especially those in her family.

The escaped slaves hid during the day and traveled at night. Sometimes they were almost caught, but Harriet's quick thinking helped the slaves go undiscovered. Often she wore disguises so no one from her slave past would recognize her.

PENNSYLVANIA

Philadelphia

NEW JERSEY

Wilmington

MARYLAND

Camden

DELAWARE

Bucktown

Harriet Tubman's escape route from Maryland to Pennsylvania

In nineteen trips, Harriet rescued more than three hundred slaves. Harriet said, "On my Underground Railroad, I never ran my train off the track and I never lost a passenger."

During the Civil War, Harriet served as a nurse, a spy, a scout, and a cook. Once Harriet led a raid in Florida that freed 750 slaves! She worked hard to feed and clothe the slaves she helped free.

After the war, Harriet moved to Auburn, New York. There she raised money to help freed slaves. She gave talks about her slave days and her work as a conductor on the Underground Railroad. Harriet couldn't read or write, but she told her story to a woman named Sarah Bradford. Sarah wrote a book called *Scenes in the Life of Harriet Tubman*. Harriet used money from the book to buy her home and to open a home for elderly African-Americans.

Harriet Tubman died on March 10, 1913, when she was more than ninety years old. A marker on her grave praises Harriet's brave work that led so many of her people to freedom.

Harriet Tubman's home in Auburn, New York

Sitting Bull

1831–1890

Sitting Bull was born in a tepee on the banks of the Missouri River in the Dakota Territory. The time was probably March 1831. This is the month Sitting Bull's Lakota Sioux tribe called "The-Winter-When-Yellow-Eyes-Played-in-the-Snow."

Her-Holy-Door, Sitting Bull's mother, wrapped him in a soft, warm fur. His father, Returns Again, proudly told family and friends about his son's birth.

His parents called their lively baby Jumping Badger.

Jumping Badger watched everything in his world. He saw his mother cooking and his father making arrows. He enjoyed seeing the wind ripple the prairie grass. He watched his people as they worked, sang, danced, laughed, swam, raced, and wrestled.

Jumping Badger was slow and deliberate in everything he did, so his parents nicknamed him Hunkesni, or Slow.

Slow was a loving name for a boy who looked and thought before he did something.

Slow especially liked horses. When he was three years old, Slow could ride a horse. Two years later, he had his own horse. When he was seven, his father trusted him to care for the family's valuable horse herd.

The world was Slow's school. His parents and relatives taught him the skills he needed to become a Lakota warrior. He learned how to make a bow and to chip stone arrowheads. He learned how to hunt antelope, deer, and buffalo. Sitting Bull said, "When I was ten years old, I was famous as a hunter." This is when he killed his first buffalo.

Horse

Slow learned to be kind, to ignore pain, and to fearlessly face death.

Slow trained to be the fastest runner, strongest swimmer, and best shot. His favorite games were the Hoop Game, where he shot arrows through a rolling hoop, and Throwing Them Off Their Horses, where he tried to knock his friends off their horses.

Slow dreamed of becoming a brave warrior like his father. One day, Slow trailed his father, who was going to fight some enemies. His father was angry when he discovered that his son had followed him, but he let Slow join the fight. During the battle, Slow "counted coup," or touched an enemy, for the first time. To count coup was a very brave thing to do because Slow had to ride close enough to his enemy to touch him with a stick.

To honor this act, Slow was given a new name: Sitting Bull.

Sitting Bull, a skilled leader, became a warrior feared by his enemies. He was also a talented singer who created many battle and hunting songs. Sitting Bull became a kind man who gave away many gifts, especially to children.

As Sitting Bull grew up, Americans traveled through, then settled on the lands of the Lakota. Sitting Bull kept away from the Americans at first, but by 1864 that became impossible. The Americans were taking too much Lakota land.

Buffalo

Sitting Bull led attacks on American wagon trains, pioneers, and soldiers. He warned the Americans to stay away from Lakota land. If the Americans left, he would stop attacking. Sitting Bull said, "Even a bird will defend its nest."

Many Native Americans followed Sitting Bull to defend their homeland. When a railroad was built across Lakota land, more battles were fought. In 1876, President Ulysses S. Grant ordered Sitting Bull and other Native Americans onto reservations.

Sitting Bull refused to leave the land he loved. General George Armstrong Custer went to force Sitting Bull onto the reservation. Sitting Bull urged his people to fight back if attacked.

Custer and his army attacked Sitting Bull's camp along the Little Big Horn River on June 25, 1876. Sitting Bull, who was now a holy man, didn't join the fight. Crazy Horse, another Lakota warrior, led the Native Americans against General Custer. All of the U.S. soldiers, including General Custer, died in the Battle of Little Big Horn.

The victorious Native Americans split into small groups and scattered to find safety. Sitting Bull and his band escaped to Canada. Sitting Bull knew that the U.S. Army was too powerful to defeat.

Sitting Bull's headdress

Five years later, hunger, sickness, and cold forced Sitting Bull to return to the United States. On July 19, 1881, he surrendered, saying, "I wish it to be remembered that I was the last of my tribe to surrender my rifle."

Sitting Bull remained a leader on the Standing Rock Reservation in South Dakota. People came to see him and talk with him about Lakota life. Sitting Bull became famous around the world.

In 1885, Buffalo Bill Cody invited Sitting Bull to join his Wild West Show. More than six thousand people saw Sitting Bull's first show in New York City. Sitting Bull soon grew tired of the show. He wanted to be home on his beloved prairie, so he returned to Standing Rock.

Buffalo Bill Cody

In December 1890, Sitting Bull decided to go to the Pine Ridge Reservation for a special ceremony. Pine Ridge was south of Standing Rock. Major James McLaughlin told Sitting Bull he could not go to Pine Ridge. He was afraid Sitting Bull might try to lead a Native American uprising. Major McLaughlin ordered his Lakota policemen to arrest Sitting Bull. Before he could leave, however, Sitting Bull was shot and killed.

Sitting Bull was buried near Mobridge, South Dakota, on the banks of the Missouri River, where he was born fifty-nine years earlier. Today a tall statue of Sitting Bull gazes out over the world he loved so much and fought so hard to save.

BUFFALO BILL'S
WILD WEST

Thomas Edison

1842–1931

The page in the family Bible listing the births of the Edison children was almost full. There was just enough space at the bottom for Samuel Edison to squeeze in his last son's name: Thomas Alva Edison — February 11, 1847.

Thomas

Thomas was a happy, curious child. He giggled and laughed as if he knew a joke no one else knew. Smiling, Thomas watched his family read, sew, play games, draw, talk, and work.

As he grew older, Thomas enjoyed exploring his world of Milan, Ohio. He stared down his backyard hill at the busy shipyards below. Men loaded boats, wagons rumbled, and sailors sang.

While he studied the world, Thomas ran his fingers through his hair and tugged on his right eyebrow. Thomas Edison kept these habits all his life.

When Thomas couldn't figure something out himself, he asked questions. His patient mother didn't mind answering Thomas's many questions. She knew Thomas was unusually bright.

Sometimes Thomas's curiosity got him into trouble. One day, he watched a goose sitting on her eggs. Thomas tried an experiment. He sat on some eggs, too. The eggs didn't hatch—they broke! Another time, Thomas was curious about how birds flew. He knew birds liked worms and birds could fly, so Thomas mixed worms in water. He begged a friend to drink his flying mixture. But his friend didn't fly. She ended up getting sick.

A goose sitting on her eggs

The Edisons moved to Port Huron, Michigan. When he was eight, Thomas went to school. His teacher didn't like the boy's many questions. He thought something was wrong with Thomas's brain. When Thomas's mother heard what the teacher said, she got very angry. She took Thomas out of school and taught him herself. Thomas Edison never returned to school.

Thomas loved to read. He read college books when he was ten. He even tried to read every book in the Detroit Public Library, shelf by shelf!

Thomas liked to experiment with chemicals, magnets, and electricity. His parents let him make a laboratory in his bedroom. When one of his experiments exploded, his mother ordered him to move the lab to the basement.

Mrs. Edison was worried that a friend might accidentally drink some of Thomas's chemicals. She told Thomas to label his two hundred bottles of chemicals. He labeled each bottle with the word *poison* and decorated them with a skull and crossbones. Thomas knew what was in each bottle because he had memorized the contents!

Thomas became interested in the telegraph, which used electricity to send messages over a wire. The messages were in Morse code, a system of electric signals that represented letters, which could be used to spell words. Messages could be sent quickly over telegraph wires across America.

Some of Thomas's chemicals

Telegraph machine

Thomas easily mastered Morse code. He stretched his own telegraph wire to a friend's house. The boys sent messages back and forth until a cow tripped over their wire and ruined their telegraph.

When Thomas was twelve, he sold newspapers, fruit, and candy on a train. He used the money he earned to buy more equipment and chemicals for his experiments. He also wrote and printed his own newspaper while riding on the train.

The conductor, however, got angry with Thomas one day and threw the boy's equipment off the train. Then he hit Thomas in the head and threw Thomas off, too! Thomas felt something snap in his ears. Thomas lost some of his hearing.

When Thomas was fifteen, he saved a little boy from being hit by a train. The boy's father gave Thomas a telegraph job as a reward. Thomas got even faster with his Morse code because he trained his fingers to feel the vibrating sounds his ears no longer heard.

Thomas continued experimenting. He invented a vote-counting machine. He created a fast machine to track stock prices. Much to his surprise, a company bought his stock machine for forty thousand dollars! Thomas quit his job, bought more equipment, and did more experiments. He opened a lab in Menlo Park, New Jersey, and hired dozens of men to help him experiment.

Because he was partially deaf, Thomas was interested in how vibrations made sounds. After many experiments, he invented a machine called a phonograph to reproduce sound. Thomas recorded himself saying, "Mary had a little lamb." This was the first time in history a human voice had been recorded!

Thomas turned his attention to light. People had gas lamps to light their streets and homes. Thomas wanted a cheaper, safer source of light. After hundreds of experiments, he created an electric lightbulb that burned for hours. Soon people were turning night into day with Edison electric lights.

Thomas Edison was world-famous. He was invited to the White House. He had friends like Henry Ford.

Thomas didn't stop inventing. He created the first movies. He made better batteries. He developed stronger concrete. At the end of his life, Thomas tried to invent cheaper rubber for tires.

Thomas Edison died on October 18, 1931, when he was eighty-four. Over his long life, Thomas Edison, the "Wizard of Menlo Park," improved the lives of millions of people around the world.

Phonograph

Madam C. J. Walker

1867–1919

Two days before Christmas in 1867, Minerva and Owen Breedlove got a special present. Their daughter Sarah was born.

The Breedloves lived in Delta, Louisiana, in the same cabin where they had been slaves. Slavery had ended in 1865. Sarah was the first person in her family to be born free.

Life was difficult for Sarah's family. They worked on a cotton plantation. Even though they worked hard, they had little money.

Sarah helped in the cotton fields when she was five. She planted cottonseed in the spring and pulled weeds in the summer. In the fall, she picked the fluffy cotton.

Sarah worked twelve hours a day. She wore a bandanna to protect her hair from the burning sun. On Sundays, her only day off, Sarah's mother washed and braided her hair. Then the Breedloves went to church.

Sarah's parents wanted their children to get an education. But as she was growing up, Sarah rarely was able to go to school. Altogether, she only went to classes for about three months.

By the time she was seven years old, both of Sarah's parents had died. Sarah moved to Vicksburg, Mississippi, to live with her married sister, Louvenia. Louvenia's job was to wash people's laundry. Sarah helped her.

Laundry work was hot and hard. Sarah boiled water to clean the clothes. She washed, rinsed, dried, and ironed the clothes before carefully returning them to their owners. Every Sunday, Louvenia took care of Sarah's hair before they went to church.

Cotton

In 1881, Sarah married Moses McWilliams. Sarah and Moses had a daughter named Lelia in 1885. Sadly, in 1888, Moses died.

Sarah decided to start a new life in a different place. Her brothers ran their own barbershop in Saint Louis, Missouri. In 1889, Sarah and Lelia joined them.

Sarah did laundry again. While she worked, Sarah remembered the dream her parents had for her to go to school. Sarah made up her mind that Lelia would go to school.

Sarah saved every extra penny. Finally, she had enough money to send Lelia to an African-American school in Tennessee.

A poor diet and the hot, hard work of doing laundry had damaged Sarah's hair. Some was brittle. Some was falling out. Sarah was determined to create a product to put on her scalp and save her hair. She mixed together grease, wax, and chemicals and put it on her hair. But it didn't help.

Freshly ironed shirts

Sarah experimented with other ingredients. She used oils she thought might help. She used natural herbs she knew about. Sarah worked during the day and experimented at night.

One night, she mixed up a new batch of hair treatment. She put it on her hair and went to sleep. In the morning, Sarah's hair wasn't so brittle. Her hair felt healthier than it had in a long time. Her hair was also straighter than it had been before. Sarah was very pleased to find that instead of falling out, her hair was starting to grow back!

Her hair products worked so well that Sarah decided to sell them to other African-American women. She mixed batches of her hair treatments and sold them door-to-door. Soon, Sarah was selling all of the hair products she could make. Sarah used her money to help her business grow.

In 1906, Sarah married Charles J. Walker. Sarah began calling herself Madam C. J. Walker. She named her hair products company the Madam C. J. Walker Manufacturing Company. Sarah had hundreds of other African-American women working for her, making her hair products. Soon delivery trucks loaded with Madam Walker's products could be seen.

A delivery truck full of Madam C. J. Walker's products

Lelia came home to help her mother with the rapidly growing company. Sarah and Lelia trained other African-American women to take care of their hair using Madam Walker products. They opened schools to train even more African-American women in hair care. These women, called Walker Agents, sold Madam Walker's products and taught more women how to care for their hair. Walker Agents earned good money using and selling Madam Walker's products.

Each year, Sarah's company sold more and more of her hair products. They also sold Sarah's special vegetable shampoos, heated combs, and cosmetics. African-American women liked using Sarah's products because they were specially made for their skin and hair. Before long, Madam C. J. Walker was the wealthiest African-American woman in America.

Sarah now had enough money to help others. She gave money to her church and other African-American churches. She built the Walker Building in Indianapolis, Indiana, where she had her office and factory. She built offices for doctors and dentists. She also built a special theater where African-Americans could see movies and plays.

When Madam C. J. Walker died in 1919, she was a symbol for many African-American women. They felt that if Sarah could face her difficult life and succeed, so could they. Madam Walker was sadly missed, but her example of hard work and business success lives on.

Comb

Wilbur & Orville Wright
1867–1912   1871–1948

Wilbur Wright was born on April 16, 1867, in Millville, Indiana. On August 19, 1871, when Wilbur was four, his brother Orville was born in Dayton, Ohio.

Both boys were curious and eager to learn. Wilbur and Orville's parents encouraged them to solve mechanical problems. They let the Wright brothers take toys and machines apart to find out how they worked.

One day, Mr. Wright gave Wilbur and Orville a unique toy. The boys had never seen one like it. The bamboo and paper toy had four propellers and a strong rubber band. Mr. Wright tightened the rubber band and tossed the toy into the air. The spinning toy soared to the ceiling. The Wright brothers had seen their first "flying machine."

Wilbur and Orville carefully took the toy

apart to see how it worked. Then they made their own flying toys. Orville said, "We built a number of copies of this toy which flew successfully."

When he was in second grade, Orville got into trouble for making flying machines in school!

The Wright brothers grew closer and closer. Wilbur wrote, "From the time we were little children, my brother Orville and myself lived together, played together, worked together, and, in fact, thought together." The Wright brothers even owned their toys together!

When he was ten, Orville learned how to make kites. Orville's kites flew so well that he sold kites to his friends. Orville also experimented with steam. He made chewing gum. He learned how to make woodblock print pictures. Wilbur bought him special carving tools.

Orville and Wilbur's flying toy

Orville became interested in printing, so he started a newspaper. He wrote jokes and Wilbur wrote funny stories for the paper. Orville printed the newspaper on the printing press the Wright brothers built together.

In 1892, Wilbur and Orville opened their first bike shop. They repaired old bikes and sold new bikes. They invented ways to make bikes safer and faster. They even began building their own Wright bikes.

In 1896, Orville got sick. As Orville recovered, Wilbur read to him about a man who built gliders. His name was Otto Lilienthal. His goal was to make a flying machine that could carry a man. Unfortunately, Otto Lilienthal died when his glider crashed.

Wilbur and Orville talked more and more about flying. They observed birds. They built kites with two wings. Then, in 1900, the Wright brothers decided to take their biggest kite to Kitty Hawk, North Carolina, and fly it with someone on board! They picked Kitty Hawk because it had strong winds to help the kite fly. It also had soft sands to land or crash on.

On October 3, 1900, Wilbur flew fifteen feet high on their kite while Orville held the kite ropes. They took off the ropes to make their kite into a glider. On October 18, Wilbur glided for fifteen seconds. He flew more than one thousand feet! The Wright brothers were discovering the secrets of flight.

Wright bicycle

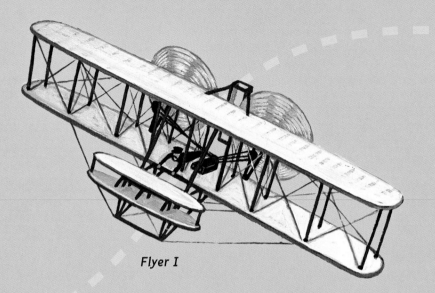

Flyer I

On July 19, 1901, the Wright brothers returned to Kitty Hawk with the biggest glider ever built. Then they set the world record for the longest glider flight. But they couldn't control their glider very well. It kept crashing!

The Wright brothers were discouraged. But they wouldn't give up their dream of making a flying machine. They read. They talked. They experimented. They built a better glider.

In July 1902, Wilbur and Orville returned to Kitty Hawk. Their new glider crashed, but Orville had watched carefully. He thought the problem was in the steering. The brothers changed the way the pilot steered, and the glider stopped crashing. Orville had been right!

The Wright brothers decided to make a real flying machine. That winter they built a special engine and propellers to power their machine. They called their flying machine *Flyer I*.

At Kitty Hawk, Wilbur and Orville flipped a coin to see who would fly first. Wilbur won.

The motor roared to life. The propellers spun. But Wilbur was too eager. He crashed *Flyer I* as it rolled down their runway.

Wilbur and Orville repaired their airplane. Now it was Orville's turn. On December 17, 1903, with Orville in control, *Flyer I* lifted into the air. Orville flew 120 feet. He flew for twelve seconds. Their dream of flying had come true!

The Wright brothers flew three more times. Wilbur flew the farthest and longest. He flew 852 feet in fifty-nine seconds.

Over the next few years, the Wright brothers improved their airplane. Soon they were flying mile-long circles in the sky. By then, other pilots were flying, but the Wright brothers were the best. They set record after record.

The Wright brothers took their airplane to Europe. Kings and queens enjoyed their soaring. They received medals and prizes.

In 1912, Wilbur died. Orville missed Wilbur, but he kept improving the Wright airplanes. Orville lived until 1948.

Together, through determination and imagination, the Wright brothers became the first to fly.

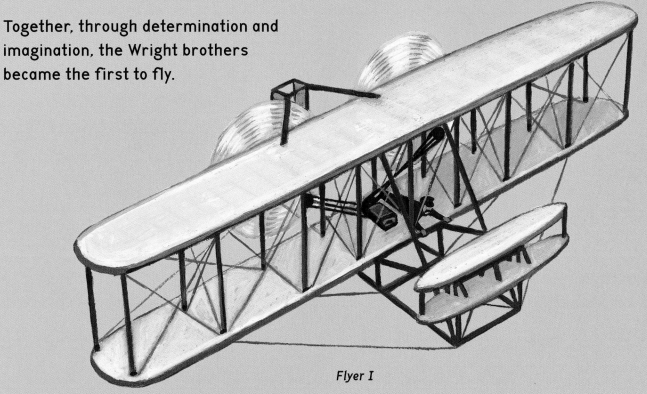

Flyer I

SOCIAL ACTIVIST

Helen Keller
1880–1968

Helen Keller was born on June 27, 1880, in Tuscumbia, Alabama. Her parents, Kate and Arthur, were proud of their bright-eyed, curious, and active daughter.

When Helen was six months old, she could say "How d'ye" for "How do you do?" She said "wah-wah" for water. Before long, Helen was walking. One day, when she was nineteen months old, Helen became very sick. She had a high fever for many days. Suddenly, the fever faded. The Kellers were excited that Helen was well again.

But something was wrong. When Mrs. Keller said Helen's name, Helen couldn't hear her. Helen didn't close her eyes anymore when she took a soapy bath. Her mother realized that Helen couldn't see, either.

Helen Keller was deaf and blind.

Helen learned to live in her dark, silent world. She used her senses of smell, touch, and taste. She smelled flowers, petted her dog, and tasted cake.

Helen shook her head when she meant no. She nodded her head to say yes. She pretended to slice bread when she wanted bread. She shivered when she wanted ice cream. She waved good-bye when people left the house. She mixed cake batter and fed the family's turkeys.

However, Helen felt trapped because she couldn't see or hear. This made her angry sometimes.

Helen's dog, Jumbo

She threw terrible temper tantrums when she couldn't have her way. She took food off of people's plates. She even hit and pinched.

When Helen was six, the Kellers realized they had to do something with their unhappy daughter. Mr. Keller took Helen to an eye doctor, but he couldn't do anything. Helen visited Dr. Alexander Graham Bell. Dr. Bell invented the telephone. He worked with deaf people, but Dr. Bell couldn't do anything, either.

The Kellers decided to hire a teacher to work with Helen. The teacher had to know about deaf and blind children, be very patient, and live with the Kellers.

The Kellers invited Anne Sullivan to teach Helen. Anne lived in Boston. Anne had been blind, but doctors had helped her see.

On March 3, 1887, Anne arrived in Tuscumbia. Later, Helen wrote, "The most important day I remember in all my life is the day when my teacher, Anne Mansfield Sullivan, came to me."

Anne taught Helen a sign alphabet by shaping letters into her hand. Anne spelled d-o-l-l into Helen's hand while she held her doll. Helen spelled d-o-l-l, too. But Anne knew Helen didn't understand that d-o-l-l meant the doll she held.

Sometimes Helen had temper tantrums. She would get tired of Anne trying to teach her. One morning at breakfast, Anne decided to teach Helen to stop taking food off her plate. Helen and Anne battled a long time before Helen ate her own breakfast.

Anne Sullivan

Anne patiently tried to teach Helen what words were. Helen still didn't understand.

One day at the water pump, Anne spelled w-a-t-e-r into Helen's hand. Helen held her other hand under the splashing water. All at once, Helen understood that things have names!

Helen wrote, "I knew then that *w-a-t-e-r* meant the wonderful cool something that was flowing over my hand. That living word awakened my soul, gave it light, hope, joy, set it free!"

Helen easily learned thousands of words. The most important word to her was *t-e-a-c-h-e-r*. Helen always called Anne "Teacher."

Water pump

Anne taught Helen how to read the raised letters of the Braille alphabet. Before long, Helen was reading books! Anne taught Helen how to write. Helen wrote letters to family, friends, and even Santa Claus!

Helen went to school in Boston when she was eight years old. With Anne at her side, Helen learned French, German, and Greek. She studied math, science, history, and geography. She learned how to speak a little bit. Her first words were, "It is warm."

Helen studied so hard that in 1900 she went to Radcliffe College in Massachusetts.

College was difficult, but Helen didn't give up. Anne was with her, helping with classes and keeping her spirits high. Helen did so well that she became the first deaf and blind person to graduate from an American college. Helen wrote a book in 1903 called *The Story of My Life*.

People read about Helen and how she overcame her disability. They read her book, heard her speeches, and wrote her letters.

Helen helped other blind people. She wrote newspaper and magazine articles on how to prevent blindness in babies. She helped older people who were blind, too.

In 1936, Anne Sullivan died with Helen by her side holding her hand. Helen missed her beloved Teacher, who had been at her side for almost fifty years.

After World War II, Helen comforted soldiers wounded in the war. She encouraged them to live lives filled with hope and helpfulness. Helen called this "the crowning experience of my life."

Helen Keller became one of the most famous women in America. In 1964, Helen received the Presidential Medal of Freedom. In 1965, she was elected to the Women's Hall of Fame.

On June 1, 1968, Helen died at home. She was eighty-seven.

Helen Keller lived most of her years in a quiet, dark world, but her spirit and determination brought the light of hope to people around the world.

Presidential Medal of Freedom

BASEBALL PLAYER

Jackie Robinson

1919–1972

Jack Roosevelt Robinson was born on January 31, 1919, near Cairo, Georgia. Jackie's father worked on farms. One day, Jackie's father left to work in Florida. Jackie never saw his father again.

Mallie, Jackie's mother, moved her family to California when Jackie was sixteen months old.

Mrs. Robinson wanted to provide her children with a good life, so she bought a house on Pepper Street in Pasadena, California. The Robinsons were the only African-Americans on their block.

Many white neighbors didn't want the Robinsons in the neighborhood. They tried to force the Robinsons to move, but Mallie wouldn't leave.

Jackie had few toys. One day, his mother made him a ball from an old wool sock. Jackie spent hours throwing and catching his ball. He tossed the ball into the air and hit it with a stick.

Jackie loved to play baseball at school. He was so good that every team wanted him. One team always shared their lunches with Jackie. He often joined that team. Jackie was proud to save the money his mother would have spent on his lunch. Jackie ate well and played baseball, too!

Jackie's mother worked hard, she never complained, and she tried to make the Robinsons a happy family. Jackie said, "I remember, even as a small boy, having a lot of pride in my mother." All his life, Jackie helped his mother.

But sometimes Jackie disappointed his mother. He joined a group of boys called the Pepper Street Gang. The boys got into trouble.

A baseball

Carl Anderson, a mechanic, told Jackie that his behavior made his mother sad. Reverend Karl Downs told Jackie to have the courage to leave his troublemaking friends. Jackie listened to Mr. Anderson and Reverend Downs.

Jackie turned his energy to sports. He ran track and played basketball, baseball, and football in high school. Jackie enjoyed being the player other teams knew they had to beat in order to win.

Jackie went to Pasadena Junior College, where he was a star athlete. He set records, and his teams won championships.

Jackie then went to the University of California at Los Angeles, also known as UCLA. He became the first person ever to win letters on four UCLA teams: baseball, football, basketball, and track.

Jackie's Monarchs jersey

At UCLA, Jackie met bright, beautiful Rachel Isum. One day, Jackie and Rachel would be married.

Jackie joined the Kansas City Monarchs baseball team in 1944. At that time, no African-Americans played major league baseball. African-Americans played in a separate league called the Negro League.

Jackie did well with the Monarchs. He hit hard, ran fast, and made excellent plays. He attracted the attention of Branch Rickey, the president of the Brooklyn Dodgers. Mr. Rickey wanted the Brooklyn Dodgers to be the first major league baseball team to have an African-American player.

Mr. Rickey needed an excellent African-American athlete. He also needed a player with courage. He knew the first African-American to play major league baseball would face insults from people who didn't want black and white players playing together. Mr. Rickey thought Jackie would be the right African-American to play in the major leagues.

Branch Rickey asked Jackie to meet with him. Mr. Rickey wanted to sign Jackie to play for the Montreal Royals, the farm team for the Dodgers. If Jackie did well with the Royals, he would be promoted to the Dodgers.

Jackie understood that he would be called names as the only African-American on the team. He knew people would make threats against him.

Mr. Rickey told Jackie he wanted a player who had the courage and self-control not to fight even when he was insulted.

Jackie knew he was strong enough to accept the challenge of "baseball's great experiment." He agreed to play for the Royals. Maybe one day he would play for the Dodgers.

Branch Rickey

Mr. Rickey and Jackie were right. Some fans yelled insults at Jackie. Some players were mean to Jackie. Jackie faced these problems with strength and courage. And he never fought back!

With Jackie's help, the Royals won the minor league championship. His positive attitude made African-Americans proud. Jackie moved to the Dodgers.

On April 15, 1947, Jackie put on his Dodgers uniform and ran out onto the baseball field. The umpire yelled, "Play ball!" and Jackie Robinson became the first African-American to play major league baseball. Jackie played so well, he was Rookie of the Year.

Jackie played his entire career with the Dodgers. He helped them win six National League Championships and one World Series. In 1949, he was the National League's Most Valuable Player.

Jackie's Brooklyn Dodgers hat

Jackie left baseball in 1956 to help African-Americans be treated more fairly. He helped raise his children, Jackie Jr., Sharon, and David.

In 1962, Jack Roosevelt Robinson became the first African-American to be inducted into the Baseball Hall of Fame.

Jackie died on October 24, 1972. He was only fifty-three years old. But he had shown how one brave person can inspire millions.

CIVIL RIGHTS LEADER

Martin Luther King Jr.

1929–1968

Martin Luther King Jr. was born on Tuesday, January 15, 1929, in a yellow house in Atlanta, Georgia.

The Kings named their son Michael Luther King Jr. after his father, Michael Luther King. Before long, his family called the baby M.L.

M.L.'s father was pastor of the Ebenezer Baptist Church in Atlanta. He grew up hearing Bible stories at home and at church.

M.L. enjoyed music and memorizing songs. He loved learning new words. M.L. exclaimed, "When I grow up, I'm going to get me some big words."

Pastor King later changed his name to Martin to honor the religious leader Martin Luther. M.L.'s parents changed his name, too. Michael Luther King Jr. became Martin Luther King Jr.

Martin was so eager to learn that he tried to go to school when he was five. But Martin was too young to go to school that year. Martin went to first grade when he was six.

Martin played with his sister, Christine, and his brother, A.D. (Alfred Daniel). Monopoly, Chinese checkers, and marbles were Martin's favorite indoor games. He also played the piano and violin, and sang.

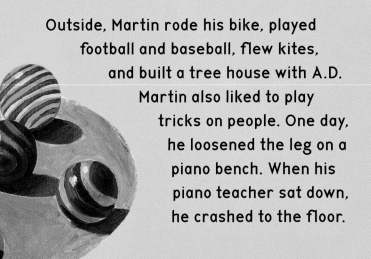

Outside, Martin rode his bike, played football and baseball, flew kites, and built a tree house with A.D. Martin also liked to play tricks on people. One day, he loosened the leg on a piano bench. When his piano teacher sat down, he crashed to the floor.

Marbles

Martin had a bad experience when he was six. He and his friends often played games in Martin's big backyard. One day, Martin asked two white friends to play with him, but their mother told Martin her boys could never play with him again.

Martin was upset. His parents explained about the laws separating African-Americans and white people. African-American children couldn't go to the same schools as white children. They couldn't share drinking fountains or restrooms with white people. An African-American person on a bus had to give up his or her seat for a white person.

Although the laws were wrong, Martin's mother told her son to always remember that he was somebody.

A drinking fountain for "Whites Only"

At school, Martin worked so hard that he went to high school when he was only thirteen!

When he was in eleventh grade, Martin wrote a special speech and won a prize. Martin was excited that his "big words" had pleased people. On the bus ride home, however, Martin was told to give up his seat to a white man. Martin refused, but his teacher convinced him to move to avoid trouble. Martin said, "It was the angriest I have ever been in my life."

Martin skipped twelfth grade and went to Morehouse College in Atlanta. He tried to decide how he could best help African-Americans. Should he be a doctor, a lawyer, or a minister? Martin decided to become a minister like his father.

Martin's first sermon was in a small room at Ebenezer Baptist Church. He spoke so powerfully that many people crowded into the room to hear him. More people came. Before long, everyone moved to a larger room so they could all hear Martin's inspiring sermon.

Martin went to college again and became Dr. Martin Luther King Jr. He met Coretta Scott, a singing student. In 1953, Martin and Coretta were married.

The Kings moved to Montgomery, Alabama. Martin worked hard to be a good minister and a community leader.

In Montgomery, on December 1, 1955, Rosa Parks, an African-American woman, refused to give up her bus seat to a white man. She was taken to jail for breaking a law separating black and white passengers. Her arrest angered many African-Americans. They refused to ride the buses until the law was changed.

Dr. King agreed to lead the bus boycott. He and his family were threatened. Their home was bombed. But Dr. King knew what they were doing was right. Finally, the U.S. Supreme Court said the bus law was wrong. Dr. King and his followers had won!

A Montgomery, Alabama, bus

Dr. King led more battles to end unfair laws. He worked so that all children could go to equal schools. He tried to change laws so that African-Americans could vote in elections and be paid the same as white people.

Sometimes Dr. King went to jail because he stood up for what he believed was right.

On August 28, 1963, Dr. King gave his famous "I Have a Dream" speech. Millions of people heard him say, "I have a dream that my four children will one day live in a nation where they will not be judged by the color of their skin but by the content of their character."

In 1964, Dr. King received the Nobel Peace Prize for his nonviolent efforts to change unfair laws.

Sadly, on April 4, 1968, Dr. King's dream of equal rights ended when he was shot and killed in Memphis, Tennessee. People around the world were saddened by the death of this peaceful leader who gave his life to make the world a better place for all.

The Supreme Court

LABOR LEADER

Dolores Huerta
1930–

Dolores Huerta was born on April 10, 1930, in Dawson, New Mexico. Her father, Juan Fernández, worked in farm fields, picking vegetables. Her mother, Alicia Fernández, stayed at home and raised Dolores and her older brothers.

When Dolores was a toddler, her parents got divorced. Her mother moved her family to Stockton, California. Dolores's grandfather, Herculano Chávez, moved with them.

Life was difficult for Mrs. Fernández as a single parent. There were not many jobs available, even for hard workers like her. At last, she found daytime work in a cannery, packing fruit into cans. She took a second job as a waitress. Her father took care of Dolores and her brothers.

Dolores was very close to her grandfather. She enjoyed talking and laughing with him. Her grandfather teased Dolores, calling her "Seven Tongues" because she talked so much.

One day, Mrs. Fernández had a wonderful opportunity. Some friends asked her to run their hotel and restaurant for them. Mrs. Fernández gladly accepted. Dolores and her brothers helped their mother. They swept the floors and changed the beds. They did the dishes and the laundry. Even after a long day at school, Dolores wasn't too tired to help her mother.

Times were hard for most Mexican-Americans in California as Dolores grew up. Many worked long hours in farm fields picking lettuce, strawberries, and cotton. They made little money for their long backbreaking days under the hot sun. Sometimes whole families worked side by side to earn just enough money for food and a place to sleep.

Soapy laundry

Sometimes Mrs. Fernández let workers stay at her hotel for free. Her mother taught Dolores to be kind and caring for people less fortunate than they were.

Mrs. Fernández also worked to make her own community better. She taught Dolores to speak up for what her daughter believed was right.

The hard life of the farmworkers made Dolores sad. She felt lucky to have a family, a home, a school, and a chance to take music and dance lessons. Dolores took advantage of these opportunities.

She worked hard in school and went to college to become a schoolteacher. She loved her students, but seeing how some of them were forced to live made her angry. Dolores said, "I couldn't stand seeing kids come to class hungry and needing shoes."

She decided to do something. She quit her teaching job. She began organizing farmworkers. Dolores wanted them to join together and ask for more pay. She wanted them to ask for better working conditions, too.

Dolores found out she wasn't alone in wanting to help farmworkers. In 1955, she met César Chávez, whose dreams were the same as hers. César had grown up working in the fields to help his family survive. Dolores and César now worked side by side helping farmworkers.

César Chávez

On September 30, 1962, Dolores and César held a special meeting. They decided it was time for the farmworkers to form their own group. The goal of the group was to join together and ask for better pay. That night, the National Farm Workers Association (NFWA) was born. César Chávez was elected president and Dolores was elected vice president.

In 1965, Dolores and César helped lead a grape pickers strike. They would stop working until they were paid more for their work. They also wanted better working conditions. To bring attention to their situation, César Chávez organized a three-hundred-mile march to Sacramento, California, the state capital. Dolores stayed behind to encourage the grape strikers.

A grape boycott banner

Newspapers and television showed the march. People around the nation heard about how hard life was for the grape pickers. Finally, one company signed a contract to pay the workers more and to make their lives easier. Dolores celebrated with her friends. More grape growers signed contracts, too.

The organization Dolores and César had started changed its name to the United Farm Workers of America.

Life for farmworkers was improving, but there was still more work to be done. Dolores worked against harmful chemicals being put on plants. She went to Washington to help make better laws for farmworkers. She traveled across the country working for *"La Causa,"* the farmworkers' cause. In 1973, she led boycotts of grapes and lettuce. Her goal was to get every American to stop buying grapes and lettuce until the workers were paid more. The boycott worked, and laws were changed.

Dolores not only worked for farmworkers but for women and children. She wanted equal rights for women and better schools for children.

Dolores received many awards for her outstanding work. In 1993, she was selected for the National Women's Hall of Fame.

Even when times were hard, Dolores wasn't afraid to speak up for what was right, just as her mother had taught her. Thanks to the work of Dolores Huerta, life is better for many people.

Grapes and lettuce

Yo-Yo Ma

1955–

Yo-Yo Ma was born in Paris, France, on October 7, 1955. The Mas already had a four-year-old daughter named Yeou-Chang. They named their baby boy Yo-Yo, which means "friendly" in Chinese.

Yo-Yo's parents were Chinese. They had moved to Paris in 1949. Hiao-Tsiun, Yo-Yo's father, played the violin and wrote music. Marina, Yo-Yo's mother, was an opera singer.

The Mas lived in a small apartment. Mr. Ma gave music lessons. He taught Yo-Yo and Yeou-Chang how to speak and read Chinese. Most of all, he shared his love of music with them.

Yeou-Chang started to play the piano when she was only three. Then she learned to play the violin. Yo-Yo also began to play the piano when he was three. He wanted to learn to play a stringed instrument, but he didn't want to play the violin like his sister. Yo-Yo wanted to play a big instrument. One day, his father brought a cello home for him.

Yo-Yo immediately liked the cello. It was big, but not too big for a four-year-old to play. Yo-Yo's fingers danced on the strings. He read a piece of music, memorized it, and then played the music from memory. When he was five, Yo-Yo Ma gave his first concert in Paris. He played the cello and the piano. People were amazed at this talented young musician.

In 1962, when he was six, Yo-Yo's family moved to the United States. The Mas saw all the opportunities their children had in America. Mr. Ma also made his dream of starting a children's orchestra come true. Yo-Yo and his sister played in their father's Children's Orchestra Society.

Cello

Yo-Yo had just turned seven when he and his sister played in a concert in Washington, D.C. Yo-Yo played the cello while Yeou-Chang played the piano. Everyone in the audience was impressed by the two Ma children, especially President John Kennedy and his wife, Jackie.

Yo-Yo's talents were recognized by many people. His parents found excellent teachers to help Yo-Yo improve his musical skills. Leonard Rose, who had played in the New York Philharmonic Orchestra, became Yo-Yo's special teacher. Mr. Rose helped Yo-Yo become a better cello player and gain more confidence in his musical skills.

Sometimes life was hard for Yo-Yo. He loved to play the cello, but it took a lot of practice. He was often lonely. His parents were very strict at home. Yo-Yo liked the freedom he found at school, where he was encouraged to be himself.

Yo-Yo's life changed when he went to Meadowmount School of Music, a summer school for talented young musicians. Fifteen-year-old Yo-Yo enjoyed being with other gifted musicians. He said, "When they wanted to play Beethoven in the middle of the night, I went nuts. It was so exciting."

Musical notes

Mr. Rose was very pleased when his student returned in the fall. Yo-Yo was more confident and willing to try new things.

Yo-Yo had to make a big decision. He was such a good cellist that he could play in orchestras around the world. Or he could go to Harvard University, get a college education, and still play the cello. Yo-Yo chose Harvard.

Harvard was a challenge. Orchestras wanted Yo-Yo to play with them. During his first year at Harvard, Yo-Yo played in thirty concerts around the world while taking classes. He especially enjoyed learning about other countries and cultures. The next year, Yo-Yo still played important concerts, but he played much more with his college friends.

The entrance to Harvard University

Yo-Yo graduated from Harvard in 1976 and began playing the cello as his career. In 1978, he won the Avery Fisher Prize, the highest honor for a musician in America. Yo-Yo played in different orchestras and made record albums. By 1989, he had made twenty-nine albums and won awards for his music.

Yo-Yo was not too busy to get married and have his own family. He married Jill Hornor in 1977. They have two children, Nicholas and Emily.

In college, Yo-Yo had become interested in other peoples around the world. He had an idea. He would use his musical talents to learn the instruments and music of other cultures. This way, he could learn more about other countries and share his love of music. He traveled and played music in Asia, South America, and Africa. He played different instruments from these cultures.

Yo-Yo remembered how his father brought the joy of music to so many children, including himself and his sister. Even with his busy schedule, he found time to be on children's television shows. He also taught classes and played concerts for children.

In 1998, Yo-Yo had another idea. He began the Silk Road Project, connecting Eastern and Western music. He hoped that bringing together the music from the East and the West would help people understand one another better. Everywhere he traveled, he used the project to teach people about music and friendship. Yo-Yo feels that the Silk Road Project is the most exciting thing he has ever done.

Some Silk Road Project instruments: a daira, a morin khuur, and a shakuhachi

Yo-Yo Ma continues to share his special gift of music in concerts, classes, movies, and recordings.

Mia Hamm
1972–

Mia Hamm was born on March 17, 1972, in Selma, Alabama. Her father, Bill, was a pilot in the U.S. Air Force. Her mother, Stephanie, had been a ballerina.

Mia's parents named her Mariel Margaret Hamm. Her mother nicknamed her Mia after her favorite ballet teacher. Before long, everyone called the active baby Mia.

The family moved frequently from one air force base to another. When Mia was a year old, her family lived in Italy. Her father enjoyed soccer and took his family to soccer games. Little Mia watched the players kick the black-and-white soccer ball. She laughed as they ran after it. Mia could barely walk, but she chased each soccer ball that rolled her way.

One day, Mia tried to join some children playing soccer, but her mother wouldn't let her play. Mrs. Hamm thought Mia might get hurt. Mia was very disappointed.

Soccer ball

Instead of soccer, her mother took **Mia** to a ballet lesson. Mia didn't like ballet. She said, "I hated it. I lasted only one class."

In 1977, the Hamm family had two big changes. First they moved from California to Wichita Falls, Texas. Then they adopted eight-year-old Garrett, a Thai-American orphan.

Mia and Garrett became best friends. Mia followed her brother Garrett everywhere. They played many games together.

Mia wanted to win every game. When she was losing, she quit. One day, Garrett told her that quitters couldn't play on his soccer team. Mia sadly watched the soccer game go on without her.

The next time Garrett picked Mia to be on his team, she played the whole game, even when she missed some shots. Mia learned that winners never quit.

When Mia was five, she joined her first organized soccer team. Mia was small, but she was fast. Mia also understood how soccer was played better than her teammates did.

As she grew older, Mia played football, baseball, and basketball. But she loved soccer best of all, so she quit the other sports. She spent her time and energy playing soccer. She played hard, going after the ball against bigger, stronger players. No matter what, Mia wanted to win. When she was thirteen, Mia made the Texas All-State Soccer Team.

In 1986, Coach John Cossaboon saw Mia play. He liked her speed and skills. He was building a women's soccer team. Coach Cossaboon hoped one day women's soccer would be an Olympic sport. He wanted to have an American team ready to compete when that happened. He asked Mia to join his team. Mia was thrilled, and she began to dream of winning an Olympic gold medal.

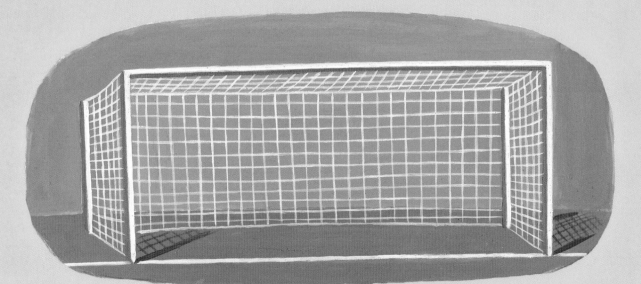

Soccer goal

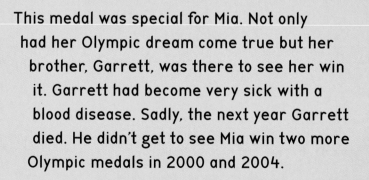

Mia traveled across America playing soccer against the best players in the country. She grew faster, stronger, and even more determined to play her best in every game.

Mia's days were very busy. She studied, played soccer, and worked out. She had a goal. She wanted to play soccer at the University of North Carolina. They had the best women's soccer team in the nation.

Her hard work paid off. Mia went to North Carolina in 1989 and helped her team win four national titles. Twice Mia was named National Player of the Year.

In 1991, when she was nineteen, Mia played on the U.S. World Cup team. This was the first year women competed for a World Cup. Once again Mia's skills and speed helped her team win!

Mia still dreamed of playing in the Olympics. In 1996, women's soccer finally became an Olympic sport. Even with an injury, Mia led her team to victory in Atlanta, Georgia, where they captured the first women's soccer Olympic gold medal.

This medal was special for Mia. Not only had her Olympic dream come true but her brother, Garrett, was there to see her win it. Garrett had become very sick with a blood disease. Sadly, the next year Garrett died. He didn't get to see Mia win two more Olympic medals in 2000 and 2004.

Mia's 1996 Atlanta gold medal

To honor Garrett, Mia began the Mia Hamm Foundation. Her group raises money to help people fight the disease that Garrett had. They also work to make more opportunities for young women to play sports.

Mia Hamm helped women's soccer grow. When she first started playing soccer, few girls played. Now young players want to be like Mia. Soccer became the favorite sport of many girls around the world. Mia told them "Dream Big!" and they did. She also taught them about the value of teamwork. Mia said, "There is no 'me' in Mia because in soccer and in life, I could never do it alone."

In 2003, another sports star joined the Hamm family when Mia married Nomar Garciaparra, a popular baseball player.

When Mia retired from playing soccer in 2004, she had scored more goals than any other player ever, male or female. She won many awards. Today Mia wants to teach more girls about working hard, playing hard, and reaching goals. Most of all, she wants to keep spreading the message that "Winners Never Quit."

Mia's World Cup jersey

ABOUT THE PHOTOS

Pocahontas This picture of the James River looks much the same as when the three English ships, the *Susan Constant*, the *Godspeed*, and the *Discovery*, sailed on it in 1607 looking for a place for their colony. On May 14, forty-five miles upstream from the Atlantic, the ships anchored and the colonists began building. They named the gentle river James and their colony Jamestown, in honor of James I, their king. Jamestown became the first permanent English colony in America. Pocahontas often visited Jamestown.

Benjamin Franklin This picture shows Independence Hall in Philadelphia. Independence Hall was once called the Pennsylvania State House. Benjamin Franklin was a member of the Second Continental Congress which met in the hall. When the Continental Congress declared independence here on July 4, 1776, Ben Franklin said, "We must, indeed all hang together, or most assuredly, we shall all hang separately." The Declaration of Independence was first read to people of Philadelphia in front of the hall. Franklin also helped draft the United States Constitution at Independence Hall.

George Washington This picture shows Mount Vernon as it looked when George Washington lived there at the end of his life. Over forty-five years, Washington improved and expanded Mount Vernon to five farms covering 8,000 acres. Washington tried to make or grow everything he needed to keep Mount Vernon running. But, while George Washington supervised, his slaves did the work. Without them Mount Vernon would not have become the beautiful plantation it was. George Washington died at Mount Vernon in 1799.

Davy Crockett Davy Crockett was born in this log cabin on August 17, 1786. The cabin stood on the banks of the beautiful Nolichucky River in eastern Tennessee near Limestone Creek. Davy was the fifth of nine Crockett children. Young Davy didn't spend much time at this cabin. Like other frontier families, the independent Crocketts moved many times seeking to improve their lives. Today a replica of the cabin stands in Crockett State Park.

Abraham Lincoln Abraham Lincoln lived in the White House from 1861 until he was assassinated in 1865. President Lincoln led the Union side of the Civil War from the White House. Here he met with his generals, talked with soldiers, met African-American leaders, signed the Emancipation Proclamation, and drafted the Gettysburg Address. On April 15, 1865, the day he died, President Lincoln was carried to the White House in a flag-draped coffin. President Lincoln was buried in Springfield, Illinois.

Susan B. Anthony & Elizabeth Cady Stanton This redbrick house in Rochester, New York, was Susan B. Anthony's home from 1866 until her death in 1906. Her home was her headquarters as she worked for equal rights for women. Susan B. Anthony wrote many articles, books, and speeches about women's rights in her home. Here she often met with her dear friend Elizabeth Cady Stanton as well as other leaders like the former slave Frederick Douglass. Susan B. Anthony was arrested in her house in 1872 for voting in an election when it was against the law for women to vote. She died in her home on March 13, 1906.

Harriet Tubman This Maryland farm field looks much like it did when Harriet Tubman was a slave here as she grew up in the 1800's. Here Harriet planted and harvested her owner's crops. She chopped wood in the forest in the background. The store where she was hit in the head while helping another slave still stands nearby. Because Harriet knew this area so well, she often returned to help other slaves escape, including many members of her own family.

Sitting Bull For most of his life Sitting Bull lived in a Native American village like this one. His people lived in tepees because they frequently moved as they hunted buffalo to eat and searched for fresh grass for their horses. The tepees were made of tanned buffalo skins and usually arranged in a circle. The bottom of the tepee was raised to let in cool breezes in summer and lowered to keep out the winter winds. Near the end of his life Sitting Bull lived in a small, wooden cabin.

Thomas Edison This picture shows what Thomas Edison's famous Menlo Park, New Jersey, laboratory looked like during its busiest days. Edison built the lab in 1876. He worked here for ten years before building a bigger lab in West Orange, New Jersey. Edison and his team invented so many things in Menlo Park that it was nicknamed the "invention factory" and Edison was called "The Wizard of Menlo Park." Today the reconstructed lab is in Greenfield Village, Michigan. In 1929 Edison came to Greenfield to reenact the 50th anniversary of the invention of the lightbulb in his Menlo Park lab in 1879.

Madam C. J. Walker This picture is Madam C. J. Walker's mansion "Villa Lewaro" in Irvington-on-Hudson, New York. She wanted her home to show what an African-American woman could accomplish through hard work and determination. Madam Walker invited many famous artists, singers, musicians, and authors to her home. Many of the African-American women who worked for her were also invited to her home. Madam Walker died in her home on May 25, 1919.

The Wright Brothers This is a picture of the first airplane in flight. It was taken just after Orville Wright took off in the *Flyer I* on a beach at Kitty Hawk, North Carolina, on December 17, 1903. Wilbur Wright is watching his brother Orville accomplish their dream of becoming the first people to build and fly an airplane. Orville flew almost two hundred feet before landing in the soft sand. Later that day Wilbur flew almost one thousand feet himself.

Helen Keller The pump in this picture changed Helen Keller's life. Blind and deaf, Helen learned her first word when water gushed out of this pump onto her outstretched hands. Her teacher Anne Sullivan spelled "w-a-t-e-r" into Helen's hand and she understood words for the first time in her life. The pump still stands in the yard at Helen Keller's childhood home in Tuscumbia, Alabama.

Jackie Robinson This is a picture of Ebbets Field, home of the Brooklyn Dodgers. When Jackie Robinson stepped onto Ebbets Field on April 15, 1947, he became the first African-American baseball player in the major leagues. Jackie played first, second, and third base as well as outfield for the Dodgers. He played many important games at Ebbets Field, including the 1955 World Series, which the Dodgers won against the Yankees. In 1960 Ebbets Field was torn down.

Martin Luther King Jr. This picture shows the view Dr. King had as he gave his famous "I Have a Dream" speech on August 28, 1963, in Washington, D.C. Two hundred and fifty thousand people had joined the March on Washington for Jobs and Freedom. After the march these people gathered in front of the Lincoln Memorial to hear speakers urge the government to grant civil rights for all citizens. The last speaker was Martin Luther King Jr.

Dolores Huerta This picture shows one of the many protest marches that Dolores Huerta led. Here strikers under Huerta's leadership are picketing grape vineyards. The strikers are calling for better wages and working conditions. As other workers try to break the strike, Huerta's people use bullhorns to ask the strike breakers to join the strike. Many did join Huerta's efforts. Eventually, Dolores Huerta and others succeeded in their mission to improve working conditions in vineyards, farms, and orchards.

Yo-Yo Ma This picture is of Carnegie Hall in New York City, where Yo-Yo Ma made his musical debut on the cello when he was only nine years old! Carnegie Hall is famous for the way music played there sounds. One musician said that Carnegie Hall "is like a musical instrument itself." Yo-Yo Ma has played many concerts in Carnegie Hall, including one to celebrate Carnegie Hall's 100th anniversary in 1991.

Mia Hamm This is a picture of the Olympic Stadium in Atlanta, Georgia, where the 1996 Olympics were held. Here Mia Hamm led the American women's soccer team to the first Olympic gold medal ever given for women's soccer. In addition to hosting various sporting events, the stadium was also the site for the opening and closing ceremonies of the 1996 Olympics. After the Olympics, the stadium was reduced in size and is now home to the Atlanta Braves baseball team.

INDEX